HOW TO
TRACE A PEDIGREE
IN THE BRITISH ISLES

BY

H. A. C.

SECOND EDITION

Southern Historical Press, Inc.
Greenville, South Carolina

Please Direct All Correspondence and Book Orders to:

Southern Historical Press, Inc.
1071 Park West Blvd.
Greenville, SC   29611

Originally printed & Copyrighted: London. 1924
ISBN #978-1-63914-604-8
Printed in the United States of America

PREFACE

IN both England and America increasing interest is being taken in genealogical research. It is realized that other families, besides those in the "Peerage," have played their part, however small in history, and that it is a natural instinct of the English-speaking people to search out their records and keep them in remembrance.

The object of this little book, first published in 1911, is to give the amateur pedigree-hunter practical assistance in the various steps which should be taken in tracing a pedigree, together with suggestions as to the most useful documents to search and full instructions as to where these can be consulted.

Sufficient information should be obtainable within its pages to meet the requirements of the average genealogical searcher in the British Isles.

After consideration, Chapter VII, dealing with Irish pedigrees, has been allowed to stand exactly as it appeared in the first edition, for though many Irish public records were lost in the destruction of the Four Courts, Dublin, copies or abstracts of a number of these documents exist in libraries or in private hands.

CONTENTS

HOW TO TRACE A PEDIGREE

———◆———

INTRODUCTORY

VARIOUS authorities have derived the word "pedigree" very differently, and it is impossible to say anything definite as to its origin. One of the most picturesque and possibly the most probable derivation is from *pied de grue*—crane's foot. Evidently this was intended as a word-picture, the claws dividing from a bird's foot being suggestive of the different branches issuing from the parent stem in a pedigree. When speaking of stems and branches, our thoughts are naturally directed to trees—hence, of course, the expression a "family tree."

Many nations have preserved the records of family genealogy in their national archives; indeed, all have done this more or less, and all honour to those who have been keenest in the matter, for a nation is composed of families, and family or individual history or biography helps to make the history of that nation, while heredity perhaps more than environment tends to explain the complex character with which each individual member of it is endowed.

The study of genealogy, therefore, is a useful one ; but, apart from such considerations, there are many who are personally interested in their own ancestry, and would like to be able to trace pedigrees and learn more of their family history ; but the probability is that they have not the slightest idea how to set about the work. Others may think (however interested they might be in *results*) that the details they would have to master must be necessarily dry as dust, and that the search itself would run away with a great deal of money.

Well, though it is quite possible to expend large sums in pedigree-hunting, it is by no means necessary to do so ; and, though some dry records may have to be plodded through, searches are in general replete with interest. The reader may possibly be reassured on both these points before laying down this little book, the especial aim of which will be to show the amateur how he may become a successful pedigree-hunter.

CHAPTER I

FIRST STEPS IN PEDIGREE-HUNTING

THE reader being anxious to trace his own or a friend's pedigree, or to look for some missing link in an ancestry—how should he set about the work?

To do this the more efficiently, and to save unnecessary expense, he should first ascertain and set down whatever *is already known* on the subject or can be discovered, before proceeding to record-searching.

We will suppose that he is interested in ascertaining the ancestry of a certain man, whose father's name is known and, perhaps, his grandfather's; but he cannot trace the pedigree farther back.

Also, presumably, he may know where this individual and, possibly, his father and grandfather lived. From such data, however slight they may be, his future knowledge is to spring—for he must work from the known to the unknown. This is necessary in all genealogical searches.

Friends of the family can give him some little particulars—all of which should be carefully noted down—and a visit to the place where he locates the earliest known member of it, if practicable, might be very advantageous.

If this is not possible at the moment, he should write to the vicar of the parish, who, from the parochial entries, would supply information at a moderate cost. There might also be tombstones, with names and dates on them, which would help materially.

Some parish registers have been printed. The searcher should ascertain whether the parish in which he is interested is among the number, and, if so, whether the published entries have been brought down to the date he requires, as in that event he might obtain the necessary information in some large library free of cost. But he is scarcely likely to be so exceptionally fortunate at the start, so will probably have to make the requisite inquiries.

Before doing so, however, our pedigree-hunter should carefully consider the *surname* of the individual in question. If he boasts of an uncommon one, as say, for instance, *Vandeleur*, the chances are that all the Vandeleurs mentioned in the same parish books will belong to his family. If, however, he is a *Smith*—well, the Smiths are not a very small tribe, and several of the name unrelated to each other might appear in the same parish. To obviate the difficulties which this would entail, our pedigree-hunter should be clear as to the district in the parish or name of the house in which his ancestor lived. But, if he does not know this, how is he to ascertain it?

Well, he probably *will* know it in the case of the latest of his ancestors, say, his father or grandfather, and let him work from that point. Failing this, a study of the family names in each district should reveal the secret.

The *surname* itself, especially if the searcher has been able to trace the ancestry some way back, should be carefully noted with regard to the different forms in which it may appear, for in early days there was a quite delightful variation in the spelling of names; so a somewhat similar sounding name, if spelt differently, should not be ruled out of court as having necessarily nothing to do with the matter, the *odds* being generally on the other side.

Even if parochial registers supply no additional details to those which friends have been able to give, their testimony may be of great importance, for the recollections of old friends are more or less traditional, and the golden rule to be most carefully observed by genealogists, is

Verify your Information.

An honest searcher would never appreciate a "faked" pedigree; but it is fatally easy to assume a certain point, and, working from that assumption, to have all future details more or less incorrect.

No time should be considered wasted which is spent on verifying information.

The searchers should not even take it for granted that all Peerages or similar works are always correct; as a matter of fact, this is far from being the case.

Even in the mystic circle of the Baronetage it is said that some sixty claimants have appeared, whose titles, though received for long unchallenged, cannot be fully verified.

Our late king recently ordered an *official* roll of the Baronetage to be registered and kept.

This does not preclude, however, the pedigree-hunter from consulting Peerages and works of Family History at libraries; indeed, this might well be the next stage in his search. Let him look through his Library Index, under the heading "Genealogy," and consult works in it which he thinks might bear on the matter in hand.

There are many such in all good libraries, a list of which will be given later on; but, while the search is in its infancy and does not go farther back than two or three generations, probably the Peerages (if the family is of social position), with perhaps certain other printed pedigrees and works on family history, such as Burke's *Commoners* and *Landed Gentry*, should suffice for the present.

But the golden rule in genealogy should always be remembered ; and, though the information thus derived may possibly be fairly correct, many details may call for verification later in the search.

CHAPTER II

WILL-SEARCHING

HAVING proceeded thus far, the great subject of Wills, which form one of the strongest features in pedigree-hunting, should be now approached.

The searcher will presumably now have new ancestors to note; so, before he starts will-hunting, he should have some idea as to how to record them on a family " tree."

And, as a help towards this, he cannot do better than provide himself with a work by William Whitmore, entitled *Ancestral Tablets*.[1] These are a collection of Diagrams and Pedigrees, so arranged that eight generations of ancestors can be recorded in a manner which is plain, simple, and easily understood. It is difficult to explain this ingenious system on paper, but a glance at it is almost sufficient to show its method of working.

The merest tyros in genealogy, or those more

[1] Published by Elliot Stock, 62 Paternoster Row, E.C.

advanced in the study, will find these tablets invaluable, as they do away with the difficulty of having to draw up a family tree for themselves.

But, whatever kind of "tree" is adopted or worked out, the study of wills should be productive of new ancestors with which to embellish it.

If working in London, Somerset House will be the happy hunting-ground of the will-searcher, and in various parts of England there are District Registries at which old wills are also kept.

Perhaps, in a sense, the searcher in Ireland has most need of all to be grateful to the powers that be with regard to this aspect of his pedigree work, for, practically speaking, all Irish wills can be found in Dublin. The later ones are in the Probate Office, and the earlier, with which searchers will be mainly interested, in the Dublin Record Office, both these offices being situated in the "Four Courts."

But, wherever he is working, the wills will naturally divide themselves into those proved in the Prerogative and Diocesan Courts.

In England, up to 1858, wills were proved in the Prerogative Courts of Canterbury and York, or were to be found in the various Diocesan Courts. There were also a large number (nearly four hundred) of "peculiar courts," which were depositories of such documents.   Later wills are all kept at Somerset House, and a great number of earlier ones, in ponderously bound volumes of copies, can also be consulted there.

Suitable indexes are everywhere provided, and the searcher should study the contents of these, under the name for which he is looking.

Let us suppose he has traced the ancestry of a family of the name of Grey down to a certain Thomas Grey of Larchfield, Blankshire, who died in 1790.

His next step is to find Thomas Grey's father, and afterwards he will trace his line farther back.

To do this, he will look through any Prerogative or Diocesan Indexes connected with Blankshire, and then go through all wills of Greys of Larchfield before 1790; and, if he is not acquainted with the names of Thomas' brothers and sisters (which might probably be needed to fully identify Thomas himself), and he has not full details of his later family history, he will also consult those of succeeding dates. In fact, under any circumstances, he should certainly, at one time or another, look through every will connected with the family in that district.

If he discovers wills of Greys of Larchfield of the required date, one of them will probably reveal Thomas' parentage. Should he not find such wills, or should they not reveal what he is looking for, he might search for other wills of the name in the County of Blankshire, and afterwards for wills in other countries, for in pedigree-hunting no will which is possibly connected with the family should be ignored.

When all such wills proved in the Prerogative and Diocesan Courts have been looked up, some degree of new information—probably a large amount—will almost certainly have been acquired by the expenditure of more or less time and trouble, as the case may be.

Here again, if the family name is an uncommon one, it would probably take less time to trace the ancestry than if the name was Jones or Smith, and here again the variations in the old spelling should be remembered.

Also, it must not be forgotten that an individual sometimes adopts an *entirely different surname.* This may not very frequently occur, but the possible contingency should not be ignored.

An old Statute, 4 Edward IV., enacted that all Irishmen who lived within the English pale (Dublin, Kildare, etc.) should adopt an English surname, to be derived from the name of an office, trade, place, or colour.

It may also be noted that a very uncommon

Christian name is often a great help to the searcher, as, if he comes across this uncommon name in connection with the required surname, the chances are that he is on the right tack, and has discovered a new twig emanating from the family tree.

Having searched through wills of the required surname (unless he has been most singularly unfortunate), the pedigree-hunter, besides having discovered new ancestors, will have come across many relations of the family bearing other surnames. The wills of the most likely of these should be consulted in the same way, as they may reveal much.

CHAPTER III

PUBLISHED SOURCES OF INFORMATION

HAVING thus gone through what seem to be the most probable wills for his purpose the pedigree-hunter may profitably wend his way to a large library, and consult printed authorities before he studies others in manuscript.

There is no royal law about this, however; much will depend on where he lives and what he is looking for, and, possibly, he may elect to go daily from manuscripts to printed collections, and *vice versa*. But this chapter will be devoted to information as to the probably most useful printed books to consult.

There are many others which might also prove valuable, and a detailed list of these will be found further on.

Assuming that the searcher, as suggested, has in the early part of his quest looked up Peerages books of Family History, etc., he may now proceed to other volumes; but the Family Histories and Peerages should always be acces sible, for he will often need to refer to them again as new names crop up.

Perhaps he might first consult Marshall's *Genealogists' Guide*, which will give him directions (under the names of different families) where he can obtain information about such.

Indeed, the number of printed books which *might* help form no mean array. To name some of the most valuable of these :—

The *Reports of the Deputy-Keeper* are issued periodically, and may prove a great assistance to the searcher. He should consult any volumes which look promising, and he can judge of this from the indexes connected with them.

The Deputy-Keeper of the Rolls in Ireland also issues *Reports*, the information in which may be invaluable when Irish families are the objects of a search.

Then, if looking "far back into other years," at least, into somewhat distant centuries, there are the *Calendars of State Papers*, with their different series, which may reveal a good deal and are most interesting reading on certain points. All have good indexes, by means of which the name required can readily be traced.

The printed volumes of *The Historical Manuscripts' Commission* are mines of information as regards many subjects ; but, of course, every one cannot expect his ancestor to be mentioned there.

Foster's *Collectanea*—"An index to the pedigrees in the *Herald's Visitation* and other MSS.," these "other" also being most valuable—is an important and yet disappointing book.

If the required name happens to begin with an A, Foster may prove a veritable treasure-trove of information; but if the initial of the patronymic comes much farther on in the alphabet — alas! Foster is of no use; for his information, compiled in the most learned manner from a variety of MSS. and other sources, was to be given alphabetically under every different surname, but this proved to be a colossal task—too colossal probably. At any rate, the work has stopped short in the middle of the B's.

Sims' *Index to the Pedigrees* in the *Herald's Visitations in the British Museum* is not an up-to-date publication, yet is most valuable if the pedigree-hunter is searching in the Museum.

Lancashire and Cheshire Records, by Walford D. Selby, may be profitably consulted even by those whose ancestors are not connected with these counties, for the information it affords is by no means confined to them.

The valuable works of Sir Bernard Burke, all full of family lore, may reveal much, besides what is to be learned from his *Peerage* and *Landed Gentry*. His *Commoners* especially is of much interest.

Walford's *County Families* would prove useful in many cases, and, if an *Irish* family is being looked up, O'Hart's *Irish Pedigrees* is a mine of information. But just a word of warning here—some of this information certainly needs to be verified from other sources before it can be accepted in its entirety.

If still considering Irish families, Pre's *Occurrences* will give eighteenth-century items of interest, but is more of the character of a newspaper.

The *Harleian Society Publications*, as well as those of the *Record* and *Camden Societies*, may prove of importance, especially if somewhat far back information is desired, while for details connected with the Elizabethan Age, the *Cecil Papers* are invaluable. They are also most interesting reading.

The *Miscellanea Genealogica et Heraldica*, a ponderous and important work, contains many copies of parish registers and monumental inscriptions.

The *Index Society's Publications* should not be overlooked, nor those of the *Society of Antiquaries*, the *Royal Archæological Institute*, and *British Archæological Association*.

The *Pipe Roll Publications* may prove of value, and, if the family is of French extraction, the works of the *Huguenot Society* should be consulted.

The *Historical Register*, published from 1714 to 1738, may supply details between those dates, while *The Annual Register*, which began in 1758 and is still proceeding, should certainly be referred to for the period required. It is especially useful on account of the announcements of births, marriages, and deaths which are inserted regularly.

Directories, which have appeared sometimes under different titles for more than two centuries, may prove of assistance in tracing names and addresses, especially if the searcher knows the most probable districts in which to look. The first London Directory was printed in 1677.

Newspapers might also be searched, for they may supply just the required link. The British Museum possesses a great number of old newspapers; but if the pedigree-hunter is not searching in London, he may also find in other libraries a fair supply to meet his demand. The Dublin National Library, for instance, possesses a good store of early newspapers.

A novice might scarcely think of consulting *magazines* with the view of obtaining genealogical information, and he certainly would not be likely to find what he requires in our popular monthlies ; but from certain journals of an earlier date a rich harvest might be reaped.

The Gentleman's Magazine was started in 1731, and, though it was discontinued in its earlier form, for some years up to the last half-century, it will prove a happy hunting-ground for the genealogical student, especially on account of its " obituary " and other announcements.

An index to the greater number of its volumes has been published separately, reference being given in it to the volumes supplying the required information under each name.

The London Magazine was published from 1732 to 1786, and might be looked up if information is required between these dates.

There are, besides these, certain magazines which are devoted wholly or in a great part to genealogical matters, such as *The Genealogist*, *The Ancestor*, which ran for some years, and *Notes and Queries*. These might well be looked up on the chance of their giving information about the object of the search.

The Hibernian Magazine, an eighteenth-century journal, is especially valuable in the case of Irish families. The announcements of births, deaths, and marriages have been printed separately in two volumes, so *they* are what should be consulted,

CHAPTER IV

MISCELLANEOUS MS. DOCUMENTS OF VALUE TO THE SEARCHER

WE have already considered the subject of Wills and Parish Registers. Besides these, there is a multitude of miscellaneous manuscripts from which genealogical information can be gleaned; but what they are will, in a certain degree, depend on where the pedigree-hunter is searching.

If in London, the treasures of the Record Office are at his disposal, which MS. treasures claim a later notice to themselves. The Dublin Record Office, in a lesser degree, will supply many somewhat similar documents, while in Edinburgh he also can effect much.

So, in whichever of the British Isles he is located, certain MSS. are at his disposal. To enumerate the most important of these :——

Records of *legal matters* often throw light on a dark subject. For these, *Chancery Bills*, their *Answers* and *Exchequer Degrees*, should principally be searched. Indexes to such Bills must first be consulted, then the manuscripts themselves. This will be rather a long task, as such documents are very numerous and often lengthy, but the result can scarcely fail to be beneficial.

Assize Rolls, which give particulars of cases tried before itinerating judges, may also reveal a good deal.

Deeds of various kinds, leases, etc., open up a wide field for the searcher; in fact, more leisure time than is, as a general rule, at most people's disposal might profitably be employed on the Deeds alone.

Wills having been hunted up previously, it must not be inferred that, when a man has died intestate, nothing further can be discovered about his property or heirs.

In such cases, where personal estate is concerned, an administrator or administratrix would be appointed, probably his widow or next-of-kin.

In the *Administration Bond*, to which the searcher should direct his attention, it is very possible that the names of the children of the deceased may be found; if not, the mere name of the administrator may reveal a good deal. Indexes are, of course, procurable to all these and similar documents.

Marriage Licences and *Marriage Licence Bonds* are often profitable sources of information.

For nineteenth-century searches, *Census Returns* may be consulted, and *Hearth Money Rolls* (referring to small taxes levied on individuals) for those of earlier date—from 14 Charles II. to 1 William and Mary.

These, or similar documents, can be found in whichever of the British Isles the pedigree-hunter is searching; but others, which may possibly also serve his purpose, can only (unless where copies exist) be consulted in definite centres.

Heraldic Records, which comprise armorial information, important pedigrees, funeral certificates, etc., are preserved in the College of Arms, Queen Victoria Street, London, and there is a similar College of Arms, presided over by the Ulster King of Arms, in Dublin Castle.

A most valuable library is connected with the College of Arms in London, and, of course, the documents stored in the office itself are of inestimable value.

All searches must be paid for, however; there are stated fees and certain rules which cannot be infringed.

Monastic Bodies have often preserved intact their most valuable records, and where such might prove useful, they will, in many cases, be found accessible. These registers principally consist of Chronicles, Registers, and Martyrologies.

The two former would be found the most gener-ally useful, though, naturally, they presuppose that a somewhat early date is required.

The records of *Freemen* and of *Municipal Bodies* may, on occasions, prove of value; nor should those connected with *Grammar* and *Public Schools* be overlooked.

The Registers of the various Diocesan Courts will supply information about the *Clergy*, and the dates of their appointment to their benefices will be found in a series of *Institution Books*, which can be consulted in the Public Record Office.

For members of the *Medical Profession* the records of their respective universities will supply information, and there is a printed work, the *Roll of the College of Physicians*, by Dr. George Munk, the Registrar of that College, which gives additional biographical details.

Lists of members of the *Royal College of Surgeons* and of *Dental Practitioners* can also be consulted.

Records connected with *Barristers* and the Bar are preserved in Lincoln's Inn, the Middle and Inner Temple, and Gray's Inn.

For *Attorneys* and *Solicitors* reference should be made to the *Rolls* and *Catalogues of Attorneys*, also the *Admission Books* giving dates, names, and residences; the latter extend from 1729 to

1848. These documents can be looked up in the Record Office.

Here, also, the papers formerly preserved in the War Office are now kept. This series, which is valuable if particulars connected with the Army are required, dates from 1700, but its Muster Rolls only from 1760.

There are army lists and muster rolls to be found in other places also. Sims (who has been referred to previously) enumerates these records, and mentions where they are now kept.

Several old *Navy Lists* can be found in the British Museum, and the Navy Office keeps registers of the officers and men, with date and place of their deaths. The ages of the men are also entered.

Universities, though their lists of graduates are published, have treasures of information only obtainable at first hand. So, where one or more of these is likely to prove valuable, their records should, if possible, be searched. These are principally the *Books of Admission* to the different colleges, the university, *Matriculation Books*, and the *Degree Books*.

These give details of parentage and many other items.

CHAPTER V

HOW TO MAKE A FAMILY TREE

IF the pedigree-hunter is wise, he will have provided himself with *Ancestral Tablets*, by Whitmore, as has been previously suggested. They simplify matters greatly.

But he may not have done this, or he may have occasion to jot down his forbears on paper either for his own recollection or for the information of others. Of course, this must often be done, and the following is a simple method to adopt.

We will suppose his "tree" begins with a certain John Browne.

He might thus note particulars, leaving blanks in the way indicated where information is not forthcoming.

The mark ⊥ signifies that all the children are not noted in his pedigree.

Sometimes an actual *tree* is drawn, with various branches emanating from a parent stem. This

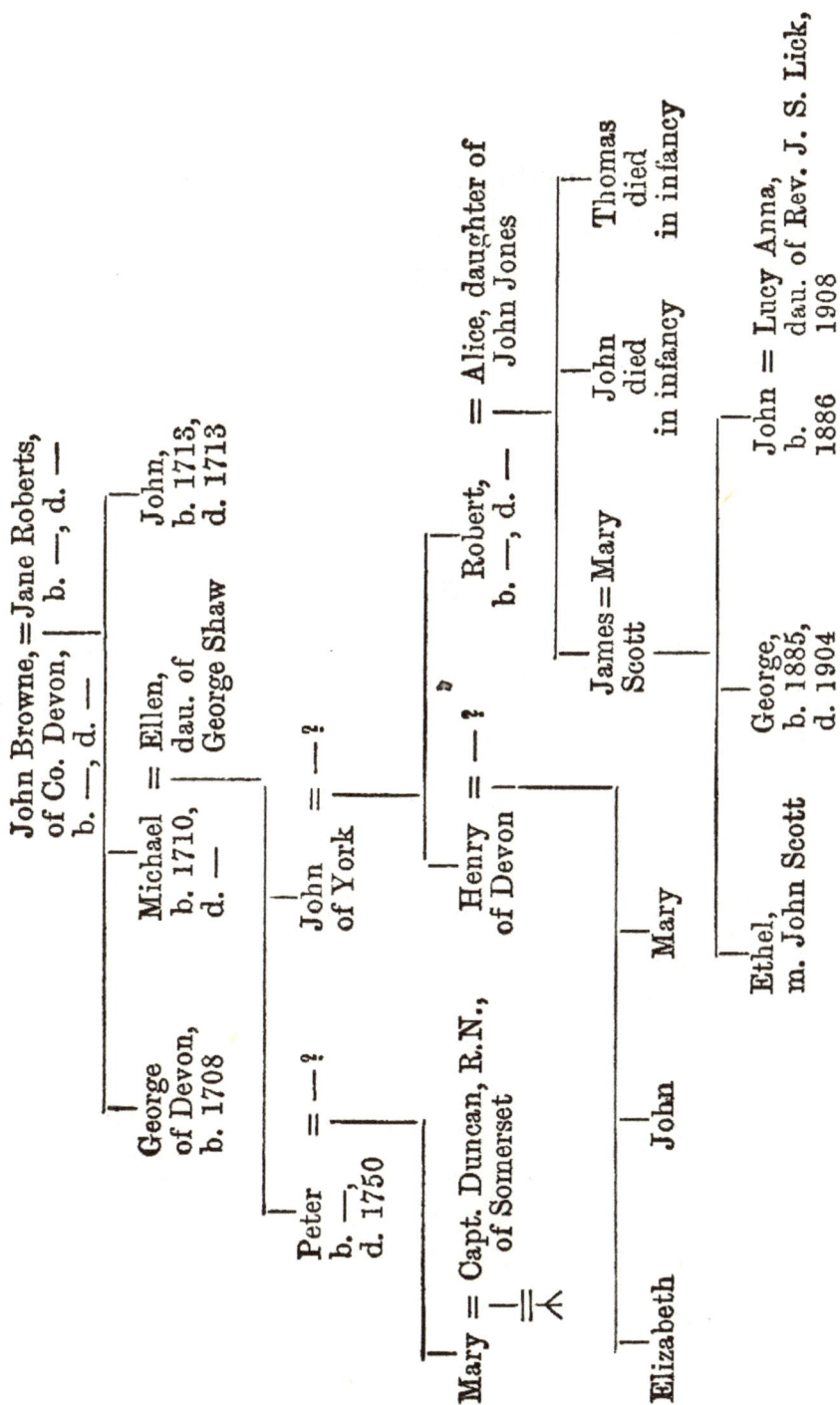

John Browne, = Jane Roberts,
of Co. Devon, | b. —, d. —
b. —, d. —

George
of Devon,
b. 1708

Michael = Ellen,
b. 1710,   dau. of
d. —   George Shaw

John,
b. 1713,
d. 1713

Peter = —?
b. —,
d. 1750

John = —?
of York

Elizabeth

John

Mary

Mary = Capt. Duncan, R.N.,
of Somerset

Henry = —?
of Devon

Robert, = Alice, daughter of
b. —, d. —   John Jones

James = Mary
Scott

John
died
in infancy

Thomas
died
in infancy

Ethel,
m. John Scott

George,
b. 1885,
d. 1904

John = Lucy Anna,
b.   dau. of Rev. J. S. Lick,
1886   1908

is an interesting method, the effect being clear, but the amateur might find its execution somewhat difficult.

Again, the genealogist may have to write more in narrative form particulars connected with his family tree. The following is an illustration of how this may be done —

"John Browne was succeeded by his brother, James Browne, who was born 1st April 1661, married Sarah, daughter of Michael Jones of Wiltshire, and died in 1735, leaving issue—

1. John, of whom presently.
2. George, alive in 1771.
3. Nicholas, b. 1710, d. — (?).
4. Bernard, married Mary Green, 1754.

1. Ellen, married —(?) Smith.
2. Elizabeth, b. 1705, married John Jones.
3. Abigail, married Peter Smith.
4. Mary, died in infancy.
5. Hannah.
6. Rose, died in infancy.

"The eldest son, John Browne, b. 1698, succeeded his father, James, in 1735. He married, 1724, Isabella, daughter of Michael Spencer of Devonshire, and had four sons and three daughters."

CHAPTER VI

ADDITIONAL NOTES ON PEDIGREE-HUNTING IN LONDON

WHILE the greater part of what has already been written applies to the pedigree-hunter in London as well as elsewhere, he has naturally, as being located in the British metropolis, certain advantages which cannot be enjoyed in other localities.

The Record Office.—Though the Irish Record Office is invaluable to searchers in Ireland, the Record Office *par excellence*—that in London—is, of course, best adapted to English research, and has the custody of national documents of greater historical and antiquarian interest.

It is free to searchers. The pedigree-hunter, on his first visit there, will be pointed out two large Search Rooms, and will note with satisfaction their comfortable appearance—also the walls lined with bookshelves, all filled with indexes of various kinds.

By the help of some of these indexes he will

probably discover particulars as to the title and date of the document he wishes to consult. If not, an application to one of the courteous officials in charge will most likely throw all necessary light on the subject. A docket will be given him to fill up containing the necessary particulars, and the document itself will follow with very little delay.

The pedigree-hunter may be asked if he has a ticket entitling him to search here. Such tickets have been rather lately introduced by the Record Office authorities; before that, no restriction was placed on a searcher, and this is almost a nominal one; he has merely to be recommended by a householder.

If the searcher cannot produce the necessary ticket, he will be given a form to fill up and get signed by the householder, which he will be requested to send to the Record Office before his next visit.

On receipt of this form, duly signed, a ticket entitling him to make researches there will be posted to him.

At the Record Office the pedigree-hunter will, of course, find most of the various classes of miscellaneous MSS. which have been mentioned as likely to be of greatest service to him. There, also, he might consult hundreds of indexes which would not help his particular object in the least, and he may indeed be bewildered by the vast stores of antiquarian information so lavishly offered to him.

A most useful book, which he will find on the shelves, is Scargill-Bird's *Guide to the Record Office.* It enumerates the various *classes* of documents stored there.

But the searcher may still be in doubt as to his individual case. If so, and he, having looked up the various MSS. recommended, thinks additional information might be forthcoming, he should then consult one of the Record Office officials, stating the exact point on which he is anxious to obtain information; probably the required document will be in his hands a few minutes later.

The following classes of documents will be found the most generally useful to the genealogical searcher in the Record Office: The State Papers, Chancery and Exchequer Proceedings, The Parliamentary Surveys, Feet of Fines, Royalist Composition Papers, Patent and Close Rolls.

The Heralds' College.—The fees payable at the Heralds' College are not exorbitant, and, of course, stores of armorial and other genealogical information are preserved there. The London pedigree-hunter has the advantage here also; for though he cannot, as in the Record Office, search himself through all the requisite documents, yet if he applies in person at the Heralds' College (this is called a personal search), the fee for information on a required point will be five shillings ; if the inquiry is made by correspondence, ten shillings and sixpence.

The treasures of the Heralds' Office are divided broadly into Records and Collections. A general Record search costs two guineas, and a search through Records and Collections five guineas.

Somerset House.—In this vast storehouse of documents the two classes which will most appeal to the genealogist are the collection of Wills and the general Registers.

Wills earlier than 1858 are found in the local Diocesan Registries, and are in a variety of places scattered over England. Formerly, if a person owned property in more than one diocese, his will would be proved in the Archbishop's Court. So wills were proved in Canterbury Prerogative Court for all parts of England, and not merely locally. *All these Canterbury Prerogative wills are at Somerset House.* Some northern wills are at York for the same reason. But all wills since 1858 are deposited at Somerset House.

In the Registrar-General's office there, registers have been kept regularly since 1837. The fees are not high. If, for instance, the pedigree-hunter wants to ascertain the date of a certain birth, the search through five years for one name costs five shillings.

To look up wills costs one shilling each, unless the searcher has a free literary docket; particulars as to these literary permits will be found in a later chaptor.

The Middlesex Registry.—This Registry, situated in St. James's Street, contains all documents (since 1708) which affect land in Middlesex.

LIBRARIES.—*The British Museum.*—The London genealogist is also especially fortunate with regard to libraries. Foremost of all comes, of course, that at the British Museum. There not only is access to the Great Reading Room free by ticket (on the recommendation of a London householder), but the Newspaper Room and MSS. Department are also free, and both are very valuable to the genealogist. The latter is especially so, as it contains a store of manuscripts and Pedigrees, Herald's Visitations, and numberless miscellaneous documents.

Lambeth Library.—This is situated in Lambeth Palace, and deserves to be more frequently visited by the genealogical student than it is at present, for it contains many ancient pedigrees and important manuscripts. Its contents are all old, and are divided into records and printed books.

There are seven distinct series of manuscripts, bound in volumes—also very good indexes.

The pedigree-hunter will have the required volumes brought to him in the Great Hall erected by Juxon, now used as a Reading or Search Room.

Heralds' Office Library.—There is a library of genealogical and armorial works and books bearing on such subjects at the Herald's Office, Queen Victoria Street.

The Guildhall Library.—Another London Library, where printed books on genealogy can be had in abundance, is that of the Guildhall, which ranks in this way only second to the British Museum Library.

CHAPTER VII

THE PEDIGREE-HUNTER IN IRELAND

AS has previously been intimated, the pedigree-hunter, if looking up an Irish family, can discover almost everything he wants (if discoverable at all) in Dublin.

So, even if living in some country district in Ireland, all he requires is to locate himself for some time in the Irish metropolis.

There he will find, in the Dublin Record Office, the *Wills and Administrations* which he needs, both Prerogative and Diocesan.

There he can revel in the *Chancery* and *Exchequer Bills* and *Answers* which, apart from the direct object of his search, very often supply most interesting and even amusing information.

Cause Papers, another variation of legal documents, are to be found there; also *Marriage Licence Bonds* for the whole of Ireland, and, indeed, nearly all the more important documents of the various kinds enumerated in earlier chapters.

Besides these, the Dublin Record Office holds the greater number of Irish *Parochial Registers*, either in the original or as copies, both equally valuable to the searcher. This is a great advantage to him, as he may find what he wants in the registers of a country parish while searching in Dublin.

But many parishes still keep their registers in their own possession, and have not forwarded any "parochial returns" to the Dublin Record Office.

"Inquisitions post-mortem" and "ad quod damnum" of early dates can be consulted there; they are written in Latin, and a novice would not find them at all easy to decipher. The majority of them, however, have been printed in ponderous old volumes, which can be studied by all interested.

The pedigree-hunter should go through as many indexes of documents as he can during his visits to this Record Office on the chance of coming across something new and valuable.

There are bookcases lined with volumes of indexes round the walls of the Search Room, and others, such as those required for Chancery and Exchequer Bills—known as "Bill Books"— will be given to him on application.

Though so much is discoverable at the Record Office, the Dublin searcher must not confine his attention to it, as there are other treasure-houses in that metropolis also.

He should certainly make his way to the Registry of Deeds in King's Inn, for there he will be sure to have valuable finds, and he can search in the office all day long on payment of two shillings and sixpence.

Indeed, the pedigree-hunter will be more than surprised at the number of deeds under each name which the copious indexes display, and as a separate index is issued (for each letter of the alphabet) for every few years, a long time might be profitably spent in the Search Room of the Registry of Deeds, and each successive visit there be increasingly beneficial.

Therefore the searcher in Ireland must not forget to devote his attention to the Registry of Deeds, King's Inn, Dublin.

Nor should he fail to visit Trinity College, where he can peruse *Matriculation Entries*, which supply the father's name and other particulars, to his heart's content. No fees are charged for such investigations.

And if the inquiries he wishes to make relate to early times, he may find there also *pedigrees* of value, for fairly early pedigrees of Anglo-Irish families, as well as other similar documents of interest and importance, are preserved in T. C. D.

At the Castle, Dublin, he can visit the *College of Arms*, Ulster's Office, which, of course contains a vast store of genealogical and armorial information.

The Betham MSS. are among the most important of such documents stored there.

But pedigree-hunters are not admitted far into these hallowed precincts; indeed, they are seldom now allowed to make personal searches, as officials undertake the desired investigations for stated fees.

The searcher may derive considerable benefit from visits to the principal Dublin libraries.

The *National Library* contains the published works already recommended, and has a most valuable stock of newspapers, some of which date from far back in the eighteenth century. Besides this, the indexes will show several out-of-print pamphlets and other papers of interest to the genealogist.

Trinity College Library is of world-wide renown, being one of the five British libraries to which a copy of every published book must be sent. It possesses certain valuable illuminated MS. treasures relating to early Irish history and ancient Irish families. Some noticeable Irish wills are also here deposited. The library, as such, is not open to the public; special permission *may*, however, be given to read there, if approved by the authorities.

At *Christ Church Cathedral* a certain number of ancient deeds and other documents have been preserved; particulars as to these can be found in the *Reports* of the Deputy-Keeper.

These are the principal places in the Irish metropolis where genealogical information can be obtained, and some of them may be found by the searcher to be genuine treasure-houses. This is especially the case with the Irish Record Office, which, as we have seen, preserves most valuable documents of all descriptions.

But if any desirable *Parochial Registers* are not procurable there, application should be made to the rectors of the parishes in question.

The publications of the *Parish Register Society of Dublin* might be consulted. The *Irish Association for the Preservation of the Memorials of the Dead* has issued certain volumes which are most valuable, as they record and reproduce the inscriptions on many old Irish tombstones. The *Journal of the Royal Society of Antiquaries of Ireland*, and the *Journal of the Cork Historical and Archæological Society*, should also prove valuable to the searcher in Ireland.

CHAPTER VIII

THE PEDIGREE-HUNTER IN SCOTLAND AND THE PROVINCES

THE genealogist in Scotland will naturally direct his steps to Edinburgh, where his happy hunting-ground will be the Old Register House.

This, however, is not thrown open to all comers in the hospitable manner experienced at the London Record Office, and application must be made by the genealogist for a special permit allowing him to make investigations in the Historical Search Department.

The General Register House consists of three buildings, and is divided into the Old Register House and the New Register House.

Amongst the important records kept there, the following may be especially mentioned :—

Crown Writs.—These are similar to English Letters-Patent. An earlier series of these are known as Privy Seals, and date from 1498.

The Register of the Great Seal, containing various records from 1315.

Exchequer Records, dating from 1474, deal with matters relating to revenue, rentals of townlands, etc., and may disclose points of interest to the pedigree-hunter.

Privy Council Records.—These are of varied character and importance. They consist of Acts, Warrants, State Papers, Royal Letters, etc.

Last, though possibly to the genealogist they may be the most important of all, we must mention

The Sasine Records.—By means of these the history of real property in Scotland can be traced much more fully than is generally possible in England or Ireland. The name " Sasine " is the Scottish equivalent of the word " seizin "— the possession of land.

The Sasine Writs commence at different dates for various districts and for the several shires in Scotland. All such registers, however, are now superseded by the General Register of Sasines, which commenced in 1869.

Wills, which are such an essential item in English and Irish pedigree-hunting, are not quite so important in connection with Scottish families, for up to 1874 a Scotsman could not devise land, so his will could only deal with personalty. Still, of course, wills must be looked up and noted in Scotland as they would be elsewhere.

Neither are *Parish Registers* so important a feature of genealogical research in that country as in England. The reason of this is that there was no early enactment there on the subject. So register-keeping by the parochial authorities was, up to 1854, a purely voluntary undertaking. Since this date a regular system of registration, like that in vogue in England, has been carried out.

Scotland has, like its sister countries, its own *Office of Arms.* This is known as the *Lyon's Office.*

But, apart from the General Registry House, there are certain local records in Scotland which might be consulted.

The principal of these are: *The Books of the Sheriffs' Courts, The Books of the Royal Burghs, Ancient Episcopal Records.*

There were no Herald's Visitations for Scotland, but their Sasines affect all the landed classes.

The records of the Scottish *Universities* supply information which may be very valuable to the genealogist, in much the same way as those in England and Ireland. These Scottish Universities are St. Andrews, Glasgow, Aberdeen, and Edinburgh.

The Advocates' Library, Edinburgh, is a very celebrated one, and of printed books, such as have been recommended, the genealogist should find a plentiful supply in any large library in Edinburgh or Glasgow.

Perhaps our pedigree-hunter, when looking up a Scottish family, may rejoice in the existence of the Clan system in Scotland.

Even if this is regarded as a mixed benefit, it has the advantage of giving the genealogist a more limited nomenclature through which to search.

WALES.——*Welsh Families.*——If by any chance our pedigree-hunter is looking up a family of purely Welsh origin, he may be somewhat puzzled by the family nomenclature, which is almost entirely patronymic, and until rather lately the baptismal name of the father often became the son's surname!

Parish Registers exist in Wales just as in England and Ireland, but very few of them have been printed.

There are also various *Episcopal Diocesan Registers* to be consulted there.

Welsh *Chancery Records* were until lately kept distinct from the various series in England.

Reference should be made to those of the *Deputy-Keeper's Reports* (these can be consulted in most good libraries) which concern Wales. According to what district is required, they will give particulars as to what documents should be searched and where to find them. There are, for instance, Welsh Pedigrees and genealogical manuscripts deposited in various libraries.

The Provinces.—The pedigree-hunter who is located in any country part of England will almost certainly have to pay a visit to the metropolis, either in person or by proxy, to ensure a successful search. Still, while he is at home, some most important records may be close beside him.

As has already been mentioned, *Wills,* which are not stored at Somerset House, are kept in numerous depositories all over the land, principally in the Episcopal Courts.

The country searcher may find that his Diocesan Registry, which perhaps is close at hand, is just the place where he hopes to discover the most promising wills.

Then as to *Parochial Registers,* he may find he is in a better position to come across those he wants (should they date before 1837) than if he were in London.

Register Bills, transcripts of parochial registers, should be sent annually to the Bishop's Registries, and may be found there.

However, there is no law enforcing this, so the duty is regarded, more or less, as a voluntary one.

Consequently the searcher will probably have

to visit the various parishes or write to the vicars, and much may be discovered in this way.

In 1538, a decree was issued by Henry VIII.'s minister, Cromwell, enacting that parish registers should be regularly kept. This order, if carried out as it was intended, would have filled with joy the heart of many a genealogist; but, alas, in early days especially, the rule was often more honoured in the breach than in the observance. Still, the pedigree-hunter should discover much valuable information at the parish registries.

But besides the Probate, Diocesan, and Parochial Registers, if his object is to find out particulars about a country family, he might consult *Municipal Documents, County Records*, and should refer to the *Old Record Commission Reports* of 1800 and 1837; these are compiled from the returns made by custodians of records throughout the country, and supply ample information in various miscellaneous matters. They have been already mentioned.

Marriage Licences are sometimes a fruitful field for discoveries. In the country these should be obtainable at the Episcopal Registries. If those required are not to be found there, they may probably be discovered at the Archdeacon's Courts.

Of course, the searcher in the counties cannot have access to such libraries as those in London and Dublin, unless, indeed, he happens to be near Oxford, where the *Bodleian Library* is a storehouse of antiquarian information.

The University Library, Cambridge, might also be of great value, but it is not easy to get access within its precincts.

And, while in that neighbourhood, *Caius College Library*, Cambridge, should not be overlooked, as it might supply some desirable information.

Sundry genealogical details might also be obtained from the *Officers of the Clerks of the Peace*, for counties, and from the *Officers of the Town Clerks*, for boroughs.

CHAPTER IX

THE WILL-SEARCHER IN ENGLAND

WE have previously seen that wills in Scotland have not the same evidential value as in other parts of Great Britain, that Irish wills can be practically all found in Dublin, and that in London, Somerset House is the depository where wills proved since 1858 have been kept, as well as those proved in the Court of Canterbury, these latter being not altogether restricted to testators who lived in that district. They date from 1383.

There remain, however, the different wills proved in various parts of the country; where exactly shall the searcher look for these?

The year 1858 was indeed an epoch-making year in this respect, for not only was the enactment carried into force that future wills should be deposited in Somerset House, but the old Diocesan Courts, where (as has been previously stated) country wills were mainly kept, were superseded by the District Registries. There nearly all the wills formerly in the old Diocesan Courts are now preserved.

The following are the names of these, and practically all wills not deposited in Somerset House, in Edinburgh, or in Dublin should be procurable in one or other of these Registries :—

Blandford, Bangor, Bristol, Bury St. Edmunds, Canterbury, Carlisle, Carmarthen, Chester, Chichester, Derby, Durham, Exeter, Gloucester, Hereford, Ipswich, Lancaster, Lewes, Lichfield, Lincoln, Liverpool, Llandaff, Manchester, Newcastle-on-Tyne, Northampton, Norwich, Nottingham, Oxford, Peterborough, St. Asaph's, Salisbury, Taunton, Wakefield, Wells, Winchester, Worcester, York.

The last-named District Registry, that of York, is not exclusively confined to wills of those who lived in the district; the others almost universally are.

Each Registry, as a rule, comprises several of the suppressed Diocesan and Minor Courts. They all date from early times, the latest being those of Winchester and Wells, which contain no wills before 1660, and the earliest that of Bury St. Edmunds, where the wills date from 1354.

When noting the contents of a will, the pedigree-hunter should put down all particulars, even what at first sight might appear trivial, as small items sometimes lead to great discoveries. The names of the witnesses to a will, for instance, should never be omitted.

Of course, it is not necessary to copy a document in full, but its contents should be noted somewhat in this way—

Will of John Browne, of   . Proved in   . (Give names of Court and date.)

Legatees.—(Here note names of all legatees, their addresses, if given, and *especially* note particulars of any relationships mentioned, all details of property devised, also any other points of importance, if such occur in the will.)

Signed.—(Signature and date to be given here.)

Witnesses.—(Names of witnesses here.)

If there is a codicil, the contents, date of signature, and names of witnesses to *it* should also be given.

The contents of all deeds, leases, and other documents should, as far as this is practicable, be noted in a somewhat similar manner.

CHAPTER X

AN ADDITIONAL LIST OF PUBLICATIONS WHICH MAY BE USEFUL WHEN TRACING A PEDIGREE

CHAMBERLAIN'S *Anglæ Notitia ; or, The Present State of Great Britain*, commenced in 1663, and was continued nearly every year until 1755. If information is required between these dates as to the professional or official classes, this will be found a valuable work to consult.

The London Gazette supplies still more comprehensive records with regard to the professions, learned and otherwise. Public appointments are here notified, the conferment of honours, promotions in the Church, Army, and Navy, etc. It commenced in 1665, and is now issued twice weekly.

The records of local societies and local magazines may often profitably be consulted.

Of the former the following are the most useful :—

The *Antiquarian Societies* of Batley and Bradford (Yorkshire), also of Beverley, Heckmondwicke, Lancashire and Cheshire, Newcastle-upon-Tyne, Isle of Man.

The *Archæological Societies* of Bristol and Gloucestershire, Burton-on-Trent, Derbyshire, Durham, Essex, Kent, London and Middlesex, Northamptonshire, St. Albans, Scarborough, Shropshire, Somerset, Suffolk, Surrey, Sussex, Wilts, Worcester, and Yorkshire; the Cambrian Archæological Society, the Somerset Record Society, and the Surtees' Society, Durham.

The following local magazines may also be referred to :—

The Western Antiquary.

Notes and Queries, respectively issued for the following districts : Bedfordshire, Devon, Fenland, Gloucestershire, Northamptonshire, Cheshire, and Manchester.

Lancashire and Cheshire Antiquarian Notes.

The Manx Notebook.

The Palatine Notebook.

Where information is sought as to *Members of Parliament*, the *Blue Book Returns* should be consulted, and a valuable official work, *Returns to Two Orders of the House of Commons* (dated 4th May 1876 and 9th March 1877) *of the Names of every Member returned to Serve in each Parliament from the Earliest Time to* 1874.

4

Cave's *Parliamentary Register* brings the list of members down to 1741; *The Chronological Register of Parliament from* 1707 *to* 1807, by Robert Beatson, gives the required information between these dates.

Besides the MS. authorities with regard to the Army and Navy which have already been enumerated, printed books on the subject, especially if the searcher is not looking for very early information, should not be ignored. Of course there are, as every one knows, official *Army* and *Navy Lists*, and a good deal of genealogical information may be derived from other books, as especially as regards the Navy.

Notable amongst these are :—

A Naval Biographical Dictionary, by W. R. O'Byrne.

Biographia Navalis ; or, Memoirs of the Officers of the Army from 1600, by John Charnock, 4 vols., 1794.

English Army-Lists, etc., 1661–1714, by Charles Dalton, 6 vols., 1892–1904.

Lives of British Admirals, by John Campbell, 4 vols. 1779; new edition, 8 vols., 1812–17; abridged edition, 1847.

Of the two works of the *Old Record Commission*, dated 1801 and 1837 respectively, the latter will be found especially useful, as it contains returns from many of the various depositories of documents in Great Britain, notably The Tower, Houses of Parliament, etc.

Cotton's *Fasti* contains a store of information, biographical and genealogical, about Church dignitaries, and certain searches among parochial registers may be obviated by a perusal of Marshall's *Parish Registers*, for, as has previously been mentioned, a great many of such are obtainable in print.

The International Genealogical Directory should be consulted, as it contains much which might be of great importance to the searcher. He should also make himself acquainted with the very useful genealogical handbooks published by Mr. C. A. Bernau of Walton-on-Thames.

The number of *County Histories* increases rapidly, and the pedigree-hunter should consult those which are connected with the special districts in which he is interested.

From the *Victoria County Histories* to those compiled by private individuals, all may be of more or less importance to the genealogical student.

CHAPTER XI

THE PAINS AND PLEASURES OF PEDIGREE-HUNTING

IS pedigree-hunting a dry and generally uninteresting matter, valuable only for the information to be derived from it, or is it a source of interest in itself, even if considered apart from its results?

To this, as to most questions, probably different answers could be given. But the replies, if classified, might reveal the fact that, though those who know little save in theory about genealogical work may think it unattractive, others who have expended time and talents in the pursuit almost universally agree that it is in itself—well, if not fascinating enough to induce the investigator " to scorn delights and live laborious days" (though this may be sometimes the case), still, that it certainly approaches thereto.

Of course, a good deal depends upon the tastes of the searcher himself, for if he takes up the work with energy he will certainly have to count on many, at any rate, laborious *hours*; but the enjoyment derivable from the pursuit should much more than compensate for these.

The great joy of the pedigree-hunter is the joy of discovery, and if he sets about the work energetically he must discover something—yes, and many things.

It is delightful to find a lost link in one's own family history, and, when doing this, the searcher will often unexpectedly come across a store of information connected with other families in which he is interested. Then there is the possibility of historical discoveries, all perhaps springing from the fact of his electing to trace a certain family tree, for historical characters were but men and women like ourselves, and allied often to insignificant families.

I do not suggest that the pedigree-hunter can easily rival the recent Shakespearean finds at the Record Office (the MSS. then brought to light having lain there unnoticed during long centuries), for he can only expect to get access to classified documents; yet by means of these many interesting discoveries might be made, as well as the definite family information which he requires be obtained.

But sometimes the discovery of a single missing link may elude the searcher for long—if not for ever !—for ancestors have the knack of being exasperatingly obstinate when they determine not to reveal themselves to their descendants.   Yet patience and perseverance should in the end out-master this resolution, and during the search, though some very dry reading may have to be undertaken and persisted in, a great deal of interest must also necessarily crop up ;   for records are by no means altogether dry reading, as the student of affidavits in the Chancery and Exchequer Courts can testify.

Besides having to wade through many technical and uninviting-looking documents, the pedigree-hunter may find considerable difficulty in *deciphering* some of these MSS.

The novice, however, need not at the outset trouble himself very much about this (unless he has from the beginning of his search to refer to very ancient documents), because he can prosecute the greater part of his work by means of authorised copies of the required documents, which are usually handed to him in place of the original MSS.   But where the latter must be consulted and presents certain difficulties, officials in charge usually show themselves both able and willing to help in the matter.

Still, a facility in deciphering old MSS. is a valuable asset to the pedigree-hunter, and may at times be almost a necessity.

Where such is the case, he cannot do better than consult a work entitled *How to Decipher and Study Old Documents*,[1] by E. E. Thoyts (Mrs. John Hauteville Cope), which will explain and smooth away his difficulties in a wonderful manner. It has been styled *A Key to the Family Deed-Chest*, and is so in truth.

These are some of the difficulties which arise in genealogical searches, but are far counterbalanced by the results achieved. Enthusiasm and patience are certainly necessary qualifications of the successful pedigree-hunter, and endowed with these virtues he has not much to fear, for the driest details seem replete with interest when regarded in the light of dawning discoveries.

Nor can a pedigree-hunter work at genealogy alone; many fascinating subjects, such as biography, history, and heraldry, must almost necessarily more or less follow in its train, opening up a vista of further interest and a field for new discoveries.

[1] Published by Elliot Stock, Paternoster Row, E.C.

CHAPTER XII

HOW TO SAVE EXPENSE IN PEDIGREE-HUNTING

THERE is no doubt that if any one wishes to expend a small fortune in record-searching he may find opportunity of doing so; if, on the other hand, even shillings are an object to him, he can carry on his work for very little expense.

The English Record Office, with its vast stores of information, is free to all searchers; so are the British Museum Reading and MSS. Rooms; also the other great London libraries.

At Somerset House, where so many of the wills are stored, the fees are one shilling for each document searched. An ardent genealogist might find that this ran away with a good deal of money; but if his object is purely literary, as is so often the case with pedigree-hunters, then a docket can be obtained entitling him to search gratuitously in Somerset House at stated days and hours, as may be arranged.

The Dublin Record Office is not free to the public, the class of documents it contains differing from those in the London Office. Irish wills, as we have seen, are stored there, and the fee for the perusal of any document is one shilling.

Here again, however, "the literary permit" can be obtained; it is usually issued for a month at a time, and is renewable. But whether there or in England, no free search is permitted, unless the required documents are nearly a century old, and in every instance the search must be undertaken with a purely *literary* object in view. If the pedigree-hunter wishes to make good his claim to property, or has any other legal project in his mind—well, he must pay for his investigations.

For the Heralds' Office, London, and the College of Arms, Dublin, no literary dockets are issued; neither is the Registry House, Edinburgh, free to all comers. Half a crown a day is charged at the Registry of Deeds, Dublin, but this half-crown can cover a great amount of searching.

Where parochial registries have to be consulted at the parishes themselves, fixed moderate fees are charged. In some cases these charges may be modified, or even abolished altogether, in favour of a literary investigator; but this is a special favour, granted for special reasons by the rector or curate in charge.

Literary free permits are, however, as we have seen, issued in connection with most of the great offices where genealogical information can be gleaned, and by the help of these far the greater part of the pedigree-hunter's work can be carried on almost free of expense.

In certain other instances, where official fees are charged, literary seachers are often most leniently considered, for in genealogical matters a good deal depends on the pedigree-hunter himself, and a system of red tapeism is not everywhere carried out.

For university and school details and entries the registers can often be consulted absolutely free of cost, so the searcher with the narrow purse has really little to fear financially when embarking on the delightful task of pedigree-hunting.

CHAPTER XIII

LAST WORDS

AT the beginning of this work it was laid down as a golden rule that pedigree-hunters should always, where practicable, *verify their information.*

This is so important that it may be well to reiterate it at the close. It is often easy to get information second-hand; but to make it his own the searcher may have to exercise a good deal of patience and research, and he must sometimes be prepared for disappointment.

Still, the result will more than repay him, for thus only can his work be sound and satisfactory, and he has a wide field in which to search for the verification of traditional details.

Most of the probably most helpful MSS. and publications have been mentioned in this little book; but if the pedigree-hunter is roaming among the documents in the Record Office or the British Museum, or among the contents of a great library, let him look through the various indexes and try to find out something new for himself.   There is a joy in discovery, even if it is only that of an unknown document, and it is impossible to enumerate every work which might help all cases, while new ones, of course, are constantly being added.

If the genealogist is not a student of Heraldry, he will find it both interesting and probably advantageous to form some slight acquaintance with this fascinating subject.   The question of the Arms of a Family are of more importance than its Crest and Motto, and through the knowledge of what arms are, and have been, borne by it, the identification of some of its members may be established.

But Heraldry is a wide subject, and many use arms and crests to which they are quite unable to prove their right.

On the other hand, many who now occupy a humble station are lineal descendants in the male line of ancient and historic families.

And, perhaps, our pedigree-hunter may be anxious to prove himself to be of noble or even royal descent.

Some years ago an advertiser offered, for a certain fee, to prove to his clients that they were descended from kings of England. Naturally *Truth* the argus-eyed, spied this advertisement, and denounced the seeming imposture. But when matters were explained to him, *Truth's* opinion somewhat altered.

The point in question is an interesting one. Every one, we may say, has had two parents, four grandparents, eight great-grandparents, and so on *ad infinitum*.

If the reader calculates the number of generations required to take him back to the Norman Conquest, allowing thirty years for each (there would be approximately twenty-eight), this will give him over a hundred million ancestors alive in 1066!

This number will in reality be much lessened by the fact of inter-marriages and relationships (so that the same individuals may be ancestors on both the paternal and maternal sides), also by other causes. But the fact remains that there was only a population of a few millions in Great Britain at the time of the Norman Conquest, and our ancestors at that date apparently consisted of a much greater number, so that the probabilities are that almost every Englishman of either Saxon or Norman ancestry must have been descended from every one living in England at the time of the Norman Conquest, including the Conqueror himself.

Of course, this works out also in another way, and makes us all descended from the serfs as well as from the lords of the soil. Though the matter may not be capable of demonstration, it is an interesting point to consider.

A genealogist, however, is not satisfied with a pedigree which cannot be proved, and if our pedigree-hunter thinks, either from the high qualities with which he is endowed, or from the knowledge of noble ancestors having adorned his family tree, that kings must have been undoubtedly numbered among *his* forbears—well, of course, he must make good his claim, perhaps even to royal descent in the male line.

This probably will not be a matter which can be accomplished, but he may possibly be able to prove that he is descended from English kings—though not in the direct male line—provided that some of his ancestors were of high social position.

As a matter of fact, the majority of our greater and lesser nobility are of royal descent, and if our pedigree-hunter's ancestors were allied to such families, the descent in his case should be comparatively easy to prove.

To help towards this, he might consult Burke's *Royal Descents* and Foster's *Royal Lineages*; but if his family cannot claim the honour of royal ancestry, the " kind hearts " which are " more than coronets " may have been his proud heritage through a long line of forbears. And, taking into consideration the millions of ancestors which each noble lord has had, there cannot fail to have been some of low degree from whom *he* has been descended in bygone centuries.

Some families rise in the social scale, others descend, and the genealogist may come across numerous instances of the vicissitudes of families.

Heirs to the highest of what were regarded as extinct titles have been found occupying the very lowest positions in the social scale. Who knows whether some unexpected stroke of fortune may not come across our genealogical searcher. In fact, there are few limits as to the possibilities which may arise in pedigree-hunting.

INDEX

5

Printed in Great Britain by Butler & Tanner Ltd., Frome and London

www.ingramcontent.com/pod-product-compliance
Lightning Source LLC
Chambersburg PA
CBHW031134020426
42333CB00012B/368